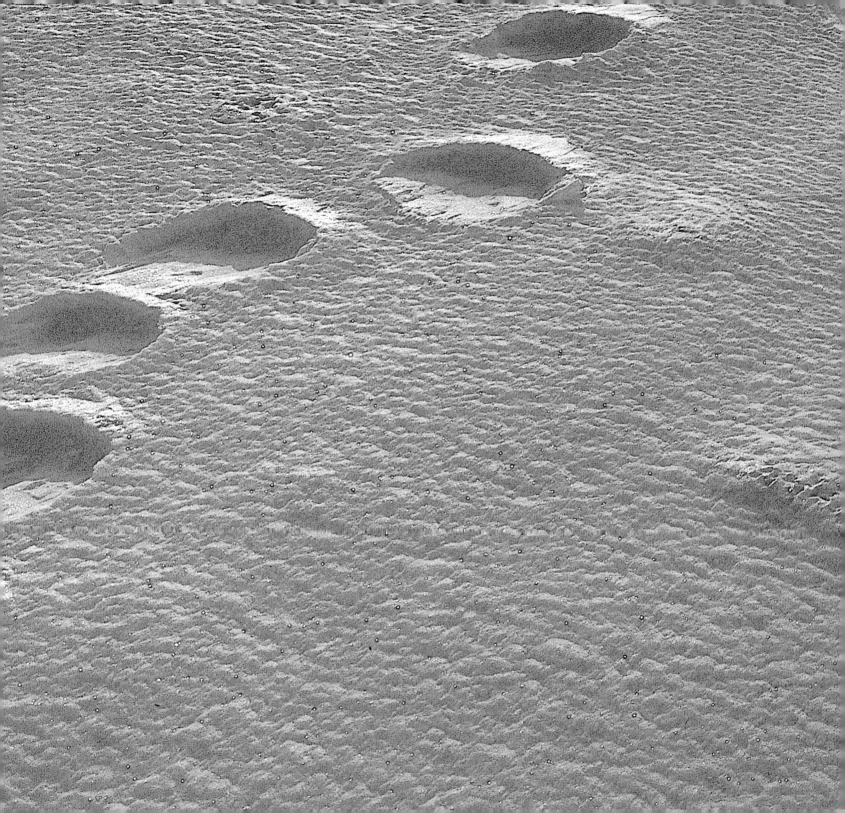

Originally published in the United States, Canada, Great Britain, Australia, and New Zealand by Picture Book Studio, Ltd.
Reissued in paperback in 1996 by North-South Books, an imprint of Nord-Süd Verlag AG.
Distributed in the United States by North-South Books Inc., New York.

Library of Congress Cataloging in Publication Data is available
A CIP catalogue record for this book is available from The British Library
ISBN 1-55858-613-X (paperback)

For more information about our books, and the authors and artists
who create them, visit our web site: http://www.northsouth.com

Ask your bookseller for these other North-South Animal Family Books:
THE CROCODILE FAMILY BOOK by Mark Deeble and Victoria Stone
THE DESERT FOX FAMILY BOOK by Hans Gerold Laukel
THE ELEPHANT FAMILY BOOK by Oria Douglas-Hamilton
THE GRIZZLY BEAR FAMILY BOOK by Michio Hoshino
THE LION FAMILY BOOK by Angelika Hofer and Günter Ziesler
THE PENGUIN FAMILY BOOK by Lauritz Sømme and Sybille Kalas

Thor Larsen

The Polar Bear
Family Book

Sybille Kalas

A Michael Neugebauer Book
North-South Books / New York / London

Far, far to the North, almost to the North Pole, is the Arctic. It is a land of ice and snow, and it is very, very cold. Even the ocean here is frozen all year long. The ice breaks up in large floes that drift with wind and currents.

The Arctic is a strange land. During summer the sun is in the sky all the time, and it is difficult to tell the difference between day and night. But during winter the sun never rises above the horizon. Winter in the Arctic is like a night that lasts for several months.

It's hard to imagine how anything could live in such a cold, harsh environment, yet many plants and animals actually thrive here. In fact, the Arctic is the home of one of the biggest and most beautiful animals in the world—the polar bear.

This huge, male polar bear weighs almost 500 kilos, which is about 1,100 pounds. Some polar bears can be almost twice that big. The polar bear has long, white fur. It has sharp claws, almost like a cat, and its teeth are very sharp and strong. It is a true carnivore, which means that it feeds on meat. In fact, the polar bear is the largest land-living carnivore in the world.

It is quite difficult for people to survive in this very cold land. We have to wear caps, mittens, and thick parkas, and we still feel the biting cold. But the polar bear is comfortable no matter how cold it gets.

If you look very carefully at the fur on a polar bear, you see that each hair is transparent. When the bear is in the sunshine, the light goes through his hairs, right to the bear's skin. This means that almost all the heat from the sun warms the bear's body, and then the long hairs keep the heat from going back into the air. The fur on a polar bear is like the glass on a greenhouse: the light of the sun comes through, and then most of its heat is kept inside.

Under the skin the polar bear has a thick layer of fat, or blubber. Sometimes the fat layer is almost ten centimeters thick—about four inches of extra insulation that also prevents the bear's body heat from disappearing into the cold air. These natural layers of fur and blubber are a double protection against the cold, and they are much more effective than any underwear, shirts, sweaters, and jackets that people could put on.

Sometimes a polar bear walks around for days and weeks without finding any food—something that would make a person grow weak or even starve to death. But the polar bear can survive for months without food if necessary. How? Because the blubber that keeps the bear warm also serves as a food reserve. The bear's body uses the blubber to get the energy needed for survival.

This big bear, which now weighs over 500 kilos (1300 pounds), weighed only a quarter of a kilo—less than one pound—when it was born in a snow den many years ago.

Here is the story of the birth and growth of the polar bear.

It all begins in late autumn. The short Arctic summer is over, and the birds are flying south. It gets colder every day as the sun slowly disappears beneath the horizon. A pregnant polar bear senses that she will give birth in a few months. She starts wandering from the drifting sea ice towards a distant shore. She wants to find a remote island where there are no humans and no disturbances. When she reaches land, she climbs a steep hillside. She walks around for some time until she finds a deep snowdrift. There she starts digging her winter den.

The female polar bear uses her huge front paws as shovels. She digs out the snow and pushes it down the hillside. She digs deeper and deeper. It takes many hours, perhaps a few days. She digs a long, narrow tunnel, which some-times is ten or fifteen meters long—thirty to fifty feet. At the bottom of the tunnel, she makes a small cave. When she is finished digging, she lies down in the cave to rest. Soon the drifting snow will close the den's entrance and leave it completely hidden.

It gets very cold outside as the long night of the Arctic winter approaches. Sometimes there are fierce storms. Ice-cold winds sweep the frozen ground and pile up new snowdrifts. But in the polar bear den it is warm and cozy. The thick snow around the den protects the female polar bear from the harsh Arctic night. She can rest and sleep.

Then, around Christmas or New Year's, when the Arctic night is coldest and darkest, something exciting happens in the snow den. The female polar bear gives birth. Normally, two cubs are born, but sometimes only one cub is. Very rarely, a polar bear will give birth to three small cubs.

The cubs are very small. Each of them weighs no more than a three-week-old kitten. They are blind and furless, and look a lot like naked, helpless rats. It is hard to imagine that these tiny creatures will grow up to become the world's biggest and most powerful land carnivores, weighing half a ton or more.

Nobody has ever seen polar bear cubs being born in their snow dens in nature. But we know what happens, and we can imagine it happening there under the snow. After the two tiny cubs are born, the mother bear licks them. The licking is important because it helps to start them breathing properly. Then she takes them close to her own body to keep them warm. The blind and helpless cubs find the mother's nipples by pure instinct, and start suckling. The polar bear milk is very rich—thick as cream and loaded with fat and nutrients.
It is very peaceful and quiet in the den. The small cubs sleep, wake up, suckle their mother, and fall asleep again. The female bear dozes most of the time.

Outside the den, life goes on as it has for thousands of years. Along the shore and in the valleys there may be reindeer, doing their best to survive the winter. Using their sharp hooves to break the snow crust, they dig for frozen grass.

The reindeer are also very well adapted to the harsh conditions in the High North. Their long fur is very dense and gives them good protection against the cold. Like the polar bear they also carry a thick layer of fat under the skin. Just like the polar bear, the fat keeps the reindeer warm and also serves as reserve food during the long winter. In late autumn, when their bellies are big and hanging down and the layer of blubber is as much as ten centimeters thick (almost four inches), the reindeer look almost like hairy pigs with huge antlers. But by late winter, they will have become lean and elegant, and will look more like the reindeer we are used to seeing.

There are other animals that are able to survive the Arctic winter as well. The Arctic fox has changed its brown summer pelt to dense white winter fur. It blends perfectly with the ice and snow. The fox runs up and down the shores and out onto the pack ice in search of food. Then it climbs the hillsides and sniffs around some big boulders. Maybe it is searching for a food stash that it placed somewhere between the stones in late fall when food was plentiful.

Most of the birds flew off to warmer latitudes when the winter set in. But the ptarmigan stayed. It has also changed its plumage. The ptarmigan is brown during summer, but completely white during winter. It fluffs its feathers so that it looks like a snowball with a head and tail. It keeps still most of the time in order to save energy. But from time to time, it tiptoes around to search for dry and frozen plants to eat.

The Arctic night is coming to an end. The sun is slowly returning, and one beautiful day in February it is suddenly visible above the horizon again. It looks like a red, glowing ball of fire. The sun gives very little heat at this time of the year, but it tells us that the winter is over and spring is coming to the North.

But the polar bear family in their snow den notices little of the changes. The small cubs know nothing about the strange world outside with its steep mountains and huge icebergs. They have never seen the reindeer, the fox, and the ptarmigan that walk around so near their winter home. And they do not know what the sun is, even though some of the sunlight penetrates the snow and makes a little light there in the den.

The cubs have changed a lot since they were born. They are covered with dense white fur, and now have very sharp claws and teeth. Their eyes are open—shiny, beautiful, and black. The cubs are also quite active. They want to move around and play. They roam up and down the tunnel, and dig small tunnels and caves themselves. They chase each other and tumble about. They climb on top of their mother, but she only wants to rest and sleep because she is quite tired now.

The polar bear mother has been in the den for almost half a year. She has not eaten anything during all that time. It is amazing that any animal could survive for six months without eating. Her two cubs now weigh almost ten kilos each—that's about fifty pounds together—and all the food that helped them grow came from the mother bear's own body. It really is quite remarkable.

One morning in late March or early April the polar bear female decides that it is time to leave the den. She crawls out of the tunnel, digs away the snow in front of the opening, and climbs out. The light is very sharp. She sits outside the den for some time, blinking her eyes and looking around. She has to be very careful so she can protect her cubs from any dangers. The cubs stay inside the den. Perhaps they are a bit frightened because of the bright sunlight and cold air which suddenly pours into their safe winter home.

After some time, the mother decides that the cubs should come out, too.
She turns around and calls for them. She blows air through her nose fast, and
several times – "huff–huff–huff–huff." This means, 'Come to me!' A few minutes
later the cubs timidly climb out of the den opening. They sit down beside their
mother and look around at this strange, cold, and very beautiful world outside.
But the first visit does not last very long.

After perhaps half an hour, the female bear decides that it is enough for today. She crawls back into the den and the cubs follow.

Even though the mother bear is very hungry now, she cannot leave the den immediately. Her cubs must get used to the cold and often dangerous life outside the den. They need training and they must develop their muscles before they can follow her safely. Therefore the female bear has to stay at the den for several days, perhaps a week or more. She must allow the cubs to play, jump, and run so that they become strong and fast.

Every day the cubs spend more time outside the den. The female lies still in the sun. But her cubs get more and more courageous. They run after each other, slide down the hillside, and climb up again. They play "hide-and-seek" behind their mother, or they play "king of the castle" on a small snow pile. Soon they get tired, and want to suckle their mother. She often sits up like a human being with the cubs on her lap and with her two strong front paws around them. After rest and food, the cubs are refreshed, and start to play again. Sometimes they try to tease their mother to join them in the play, but she only wants to rest and sleep.

In April the sun rises clear above the horizon. From now on, it will stay in the sky day and night for several months. The polar bear female decides that it is time to leave the den for good. She climbs down the hillside and turns to the cubs. "Huff-huff-huff-huff!" 'Follow me!' she says. And the cubs slide down towards her. They jump around and play on their way towards the shore and the sea ice. If we were to watch them from a nearby hill, we would see them for an hour or two, the mother first and the two cubs trailing after her. But then we would lose sight of them. The polar bear family will never return to this winter home again.

It must be exciting for the cubs to come out on the sea ice for the first time. Maybe they will meet a huge walrus resting on the ice. Perhaps they will be frightened because the walrus is really big. It weighs a ton and a half, and it has long tusks sticking out of its mouth. The mother bear knows that the walrus can be dangerous, and she and her cubs will make a wide circle around it.

The polar bears see large flocks of seabirds flying low over the ice, swarming in from the sea.

All these birds are coming back now from the south to nest and lay eggs on the steep mountain cliffs. There's the black guillemot with bright red feet and a white dot on the wing, the funny little auks, and the white ivory gull. They come here to breed because the arctic sea provides plenty of food for them and their chicks.

There are seals as well, and that is another matter, because seals are the polar bear's favorite food. The small ringed seal is the most common, but there are also many bearded seals. The seals are often very curious. Sometimes they swim in the ice cold water and look at the bears with big, round eyes. The polar bear female ignores the seals, because she knows that she cannot catch them in the water. She has to use other hunting techniques.

After some time the female bear discovers some seals sleeping on the ice. They like to bask in the sun after the long, dark winter. The female must try to catch one. She leaves the cubs behind so they will not disturb her. They under-stand what is happening, and obediently sit down on the ice to watch their mother hunt.

The female bear sneaks out on the ice. She hides behind ice hummocks and pressure ridges, waves of ice pushed up by the expanding pack ice. She sneaks closer and closer. Sometimes she has to stand completely still, because the seal on the ice lifts its head and looks around. When the seal falls asleep again, the polar bear moves again. As she gets closer, she lies down on her belly. She crawls forward slowly, silently, and very carefully.

The distance between her and the seal is fifty meters (yards). The seal lifts its head and looks around. The polar bear lies completely still. The seal goes back to sleep, and the polar bear gradually sneaks closer and closer. The polar bear must be very careful, because the seal lies near a hole in the ice. One wrong move, and the seal will slip into the water. Then everything would be spoiled.

The seal lifts its head once again, but does not see the bear. It goes back to sleep. The polar bear pulls its legs under its body, all ready. Suddenly it attacks. It jumps forward very quickly—two, three long jumps—and strikes the seal with one of its paws. The seal is hurled over the ice, away from the water hole. Seconds later, it is dead.

The polar bear female takes its prey in its mouth and walks towards the cubs. She drops the seal on the ice, and starts feeding. The cubs sniff the dead seal, lick some blood, and try to bite the meat. But this food is for their mother. She is very hungry.

After an hour or two, everything is gone. The polar bear female has eaten 60 kilos of skin, blubber, meat and bones in one meal – that's 130 pounds of food! She will not need to hunt now for several days.

The polar bear family continues its wandering across the pack ice. The cubs get stronger every day. Soon they are able to walk day and night. We know that they can travel more than forty kilometers, or about twenty-five miles, every day, and they can keep up that rate for several days in a row. It is difficult travel.

They climb ice hummocks and pressure ridges. They swim across long stretches of open, ice-cold water. They visit distant shores and islands. When they come near other polar bears, the mother tries to avoid them. She knows that solitary bears can be dangerous, and one might try to kill and eat her cubs.

Soon it is full arctic summer, and there is life everywhere. The polar bear cubs see mountainsides that are swarming with tens of thousands of birds. They see tiny flowers that cover the ground with beautiful red, yellow, and white blossoms.

The cubs follow their mother closely and learn from her every day. They see how she hunts, and when they are half a year old, they try hunting themselves. They do not catch anything the first times they try, but they are learning. They watch their mother climbing a bird cliff to search for eggs and chicks. They see her dive for kelp and seaweed which she offers them as food. It is not their favorite, but they eat some anyway. Now and then they come ashore on islands where geese or eider ducks are breeding. Sometimes their mother chases the birds all around, but at other times she is not interested at all. She probably knows that it is impossible to catch them as they fly away.

The cubs notice their mother eating grass. They try to eat grass too. A few reindeer are grazing nearby. But the polar bear female does not try to catch them. She knows that it is impossible, because the reindeer can run much faster.

Then the summer is over once again. The days get colder, and the first snow covers the mountains. The birds leave the land, and the flowers wither away. In September, each of the cubs weighs sixty kilos or more − over 130 pounds. They are strong and fast now, but they are not yet ready to leave their mother. There is still much to learn from her about catching seals and finding other food. So they enter another winter together.

This winter, the female polar bear does not dig a den. She stays out the whole long winter with her cubs. They will learn now how cold and dark the arctic winter can be. When a storm sweeps in, they hide behind an iceberg.

They curl up like big dogs and sleep through the storm. Storms can last a few hours, or they can howl away for days. When the wind calms down, they get up, shake the snow off their pelts and continue their endless walking. If a storm gets really bad, then the bears may dig out a shallow cave in a snowdrift so they can curl up inside and wait for the storm to cease.

The cubs' second winter, their first one outside, is a harsh and difficult test. But the bears that survive this first winter in the wild will stand a good chance to live a long life – up to 40 years.

The cubs enter their second summer together with their mother. Now they are almost as big as she is. They have learned to catch seals themselves, and they do not need to suckle her anymore. They are getting more and more independent. Sometimes they roam far away from their mother. They can be away from her for an hour or more, exploring the strange and exciting world on their own.

The summer passes, and the family enters another winter out on the ice together. The cubs are two years old now, large, strong, and more experienced. As a new spring approaches, the mother bear gets uneasy. The time has come for her and her cubs to separate.

One day the family meets a large adult male bear. Usually, the female would try to run away or chase away the intruder. But not this time. Instead he chases away her cubs. She does not seem to care. She is more interested in the male bear this time. Then the male mates with the female bear. The male and the female stay together for a day or two, sometimes longer, mating several times. Those two days of mating are the only time that polar bear parents spend together. The cubs stay nearby, but every time they get too close, they are chased away by the big male.

The time has come for the two cubs to live their own lives, and one day they walk away from their mother for good. They will never go looking for her again because they don't really need her help and protection anymore. She has taught them the skills they need to hunt and survive in this frozen world. They are young, strong, and fast – ready to meet any challenges.

The two young bears stay together for a few weeks after they have left their mother. Then one day they also decide to leave each other, each to go his own way. They will probably never meet again. They will live through their third spring and summer alone, walking across the sea ice to hunt for seals.

Their mother is pregnant again after mating with the big male that chased the cubs away. She starts wandering from the drifting sea ice towards a distant shore. She wants to find a remote island where there are no humans and no disturbances. When she reaches land, she climbs a steep hillside. She walks around for some time until she finds a deep snowdrift. And then, once again, she starts digging her winter den.

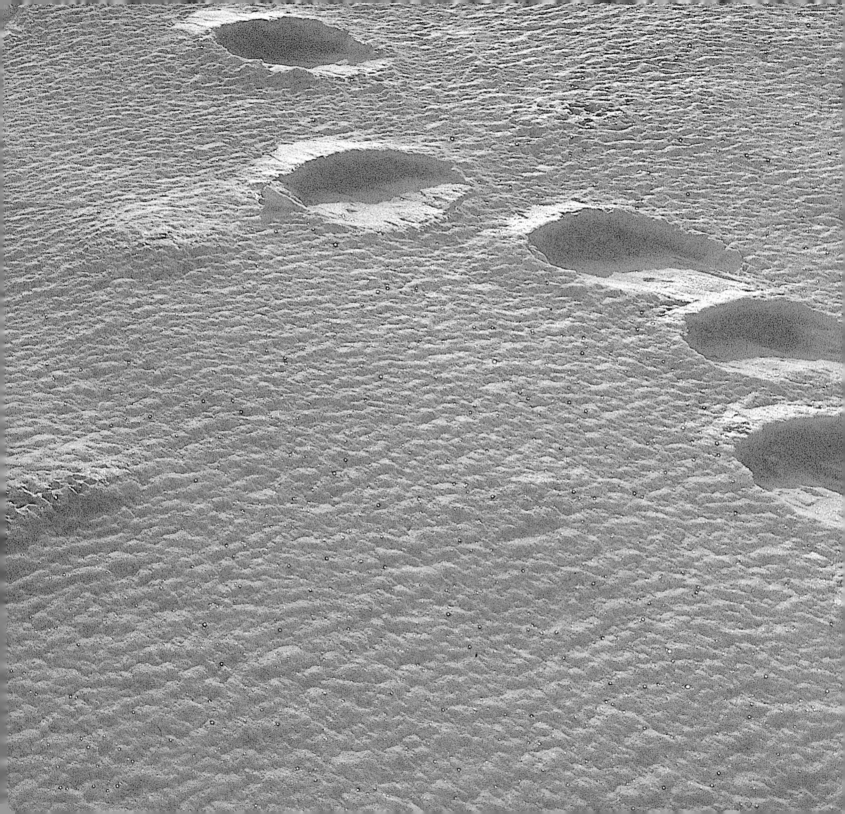